P9-BYS-574

DISCARDED

MT. PLEASANT BRANCH

THE YOUNG
ASTRONOMER

HARRY FORD

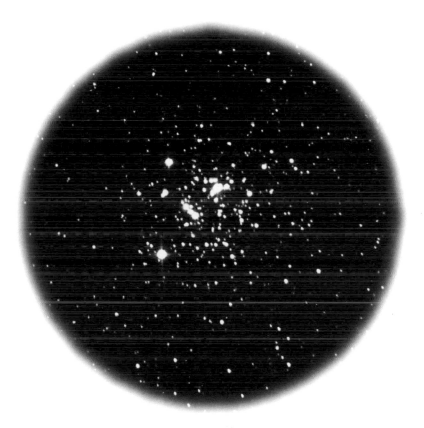

DK PUBLISHING, INC.

MTp AUG 24 1998 520
F
JUV

A DK PUBLISHING BOOK

Project Editor Cynthia O'Neill
Designers Iain Morris and Janet Allis
US Editors Kristin Ward, Nicole Zarick
Photography Andy Crawford, Gary Ombler
Picture Research Sam Ruston
Production Lisa Moss
DTP Designer Nicky Studdart
Senior Managing Editor Gillian Denton
Senior Managing Art Editor Julia Harris

First American Edition, 1998
2 4 6 8 10 9 7 5 3
Published in the United States by DK Publishing, Inc., 95 Madison Avenue, New York, New York 10016
Visit us on the World Wide Web at http://www.dk.com

Copyright © 1998 Dorling Kindersley Limited, London
All rights reserved under International and Pan-American Copyright Conventions. No part of this publication may be
reproduced, stored in a retrieval system, or transmitted in any form or by any means, electronic, mechanical, photocopying,
recording, or otherwise, without the prior written permission of the copyright holder. Published in Great Britain by Dorling
Kindersley Limited.

Ford, Harry.
The Young Astronomer / by Harry Ford.-- 1st American ed.
p. cm. -- (The young enthusiast series)
Summary: Introduces the basics of astronomy through a variety of projects, including a model of a
lunar eclipse and simulating a "comet's tail."
ISBN 0-7894-2061-9
1. Astronomy--Juvenile literature. 2. Astronomy--Experiments--Juvenile literature. 3. Astronomy--Observer's manuals--
Juvenile literature. [1. Astronomy--Experiments. 2. Experiments.]
I. Title II. Series
QB46.S956 1998
520--dc21
97-39623
CIP
AC

Color reproduction by Colourscan, Singapore
Printed and bound in Italy by L.E.G.O.

Contents

Introducing astronomy

Harry at home
Most professional astronomers became interested in the sky long before starting work at an observatory. I was only ten when I started to investigate the stars! Like most keen astronomers, I have my own simple telescope at home, so that I can study the stars from my garden.

Y ou may think it is only possible to really get involved in astronomy by university study and work at a giant observatory. Not true! Amazing new discoveries can be made by ordinary people, just by looking into the sky. They might happen to spot an exploding star at a time when observatory astronomers are looking elsewhere. Even without making great discoveries, the sky is so beautiful, interesting, and varied that everyone should enjoy it. So take the time to learn about the stars and planets! Please look up!

Harry Ford

Astronomy through the ages

Astronomy—the study of space—is the oldest science. It was vital to ancient peoples, who used the position of the Sun, Moon, and stars to tell the time and date, and to navigate. Astronomers have pushed back the barriers of knowledge; for example, until the 15th century, people believed that the Earth was the center of the universe. It took courageous astronomers to challenge this view of our own importance. Through the centuries, technology has continued to improve and our knowledge to increase. Today astronomers can tell what the stars are made of without ever reaching them, or estimate the size and age of the universe itself.

Arabic astronomy
Islamic astronomers kept knowledge about the stars alive after the end of the Roman Empire, and until the medieval age; in the *Book of Fixed Stars*, the Persian astronomer Al Sufi (903–86) listed the position of more than 1,000 stars.

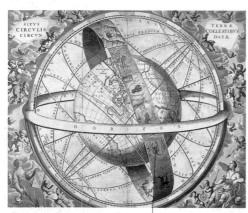

Stars travel around Earth in the Ptolemaic System.

Ptolemy
For almost 1,500 years, astronomy was based on the *Almagest*, compiled by the Greek writer Ptolemy (c.100–180), who lived in Egypt. Ptolemy collected and explained the work of all the great astronomers who had gone before him. The *Almagest* included the idea that Earth was the center of the universe. This is sometimes called the Ptolemaic System.

Early print shows how Copernicus saw the universe.

Earth in orbit around the Sun

Copernicus
The Polish astronomer Nicholas Copernicus (1473–1543) was the first person in the modern world to remove the Earth from the center of things. He put the Sun at the center of the universe, with Earth and the other planets going around it. This view was seen as dangerously revolutionary by the Church.

Zodiac constellations

Galileo Galilei
In the early 17th century, the Italian astronomer Galileo Galilei (1564–1642) used the newly invented telescope to discover the phases of Venus, the moons of Jupiter, and the mountains on the Moon.

Telescopes
Telescopes were continually improved, revealing far fainter objects, such as the gap in the rings of Saturn. The English astronomer William Herschel (1738–1822) used a wooden telescope like this to discover the planet Uranus in 1781.

The gap in the rings of Saturn is called the Cassini Division, after the astronomer who discovered it in 1675.

Radio telescopes
Rather than detecting light, some modern telescopes pick up radio waves from space objects and turn them into images.

Space probes
In the 20th century, computer-controlled robots called space probes traveled to moons or planets, sending back new information to Earth. Probes added huge amounts to astronomers' knowledge.

The Soviet probe Luna 9 *sent pictures from the Moon in 1966.*

Hubble Space Telescope

Picture taken by the HST of a gaseous nebula, where stars are being born.

Modern astronomy
Today, astronomy is more exciting than ever. The stunning photographs sent back by the Hubble Space Telescope (HST) inspire us to explore the farthest reachest of space. Astronomers have the technology to investigate distant galaxies, black holes, and even the beginnings of the universe itself.

Starting astronomy

All it takes to find your way around the night sky is enthusiasm, curiosity, and the patience to watch the stars night after night. This book makes stargazing even more exciting by teaching you what objects to look for and where to find them. With time and practice, you will spot plenty of details with your naked eye alone. Binoculars will let you see even more, but there is no need for a beginner to buy expensive equipment right away.

Wear enough layers to keep warm at night.

Keep your compass and star maps or planisphere handy.

Remember!
Don't go out at night alone—always take an adult with you when you are stargazing.

Conditions
The best time to look at the stars is on a clear, moonless night. Try to find a spot away from the city. Light pollution (unwanted light from streetlights and houses) makes the sky bright and blots out many stars. A hillside in the country is ideal, but if this is impossible, you can still observe the Moon and main stars from the city.

Useful equipment

To observe the night sky and record what you see, you will need a map of the stars, a compass to find north, a watch to record the time of interesting sightings, a notebook, and a flashlight.

Fix the cellophane with an elastic band.

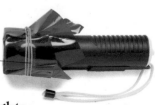

Flashlights
It takes about half an hour before your eyes adjust to the dark, allowing you to see fainter stars. To look at star maps or make notes, cover a flashlight with red cellophane. The cellophane gives a reddish light that does not spoil your dark-adapted vision.

Hot drink
Take a hot drink or some soup with you to keep you warm.

Record what you see

• Make careful notes of what you see. It may seem silly to record that you have seen a constellation, something which has been noted for centuries, but this entry will help you find it again.

• No one can say what is, or is not, a valuable sighting. For example, in the case of shooting stars, scientists cannot get enough details of their brightness, speed, and direction. This is where an amateur astronomer can be so important.

Record whether you used binoculars or a telescope. How powerful were they?

Sketches of what you see are helpful.

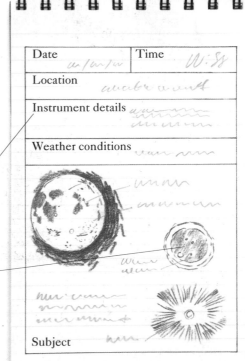

Date		Time	
Location			
Instrument details			
Weather conditions			
Subject			

Write it down!

Write down every detail that you can think of. The date and the time are especially important. Don't worry if your entry is messy— but make sure that it is readable.

Finding direction

A compass is a piece of equipment that, by pointing the way north, lets you know which direction you are facing. This is useful—for example, you need to know how to find north and south to read the star maps printed on pages 26 and 29 of this book. You can buy a compass at most good camping stores.

How a compass works

The Earth is like a giant magnet, with a magnetic field and magnetic poles. The compass needle is affected by Earth's magnetic field; this connection keeps it aligned with the magnetic poles, so the needle always points north.

Telling objects apart

To tell the difference between a star, planet, or space station, note how rapidly a dot of light moves. The stars move each night due to the Earth's spin, but do not change position relative to each other. A shooting star looks like a streak of light; a slow-moving light may be a space station or artificial satellite. A bright "star" that is not marked on a star map may be a planet.

The positions of the planets change constantly (the word planet means "wanderer" in ancient Greek).

In these pictures, taken a few weeks apart, the planets Saturn and Jupiter have "wandered," compared to a nearby star.

Model-making

Most of the materials you'll need for the projects in this book are easy to find at home: remember, always ask permission before you borrow them. You can also buy equipment from model-making or stationery stores.

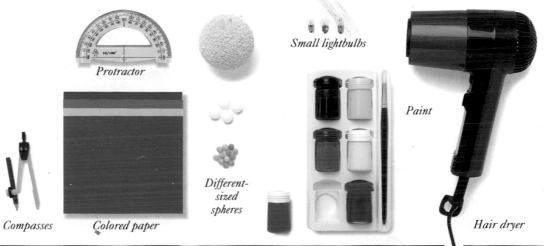

Protractor

Small lightbulbs

Paint

Battery   *Electrical wire*   *Compasses*   *Colored paper*   *Different-sized spheres*   *Hair dryer*

Looking up

Early telescope
Astronomers first used telescopes in the 17th century. The first person to clearly record what he saw was the Italian Galileo Galilei in 1609.

With your naked eye, you can see thousands of stars in the night sky. But equipped with binoculars or a telescope, astronomers can spot many fainter stars, investigate the craters on the Moon, or see the planets as tiny disks, not starry points. Telescopes magnify distant details that are invisible to the eye alone. Before the age of space exploration, astronomers made all their discoveries about the universe by constructing more and more powerful telescopes.

Make a telescope

Telescopes use lenses or mirrors to collect and focus light, making far-off and faint objects seem closer. Follow these instructions to build your own telescope.

You will need

- two lenses (see below) • sandpaper
- plastic tubing, 2 x 39 in (5 cm x 1 m)
- standard coupling, 2 in (5 cm)
- plastic reducer, 1⅜ in (3.5 cm)
- plastic putty or glue
- black cardboard • compasses • ruler
- stickers or spray paint

Useful advice

Buy lenses from an optical supplier or school-supply catalog.

- eyepiece lens—brings the image into focus in the space between the eyepiece and your eyeball. We used 50-mm focus, 35-mm diameter.

- objective lens—sends the image down the telescope tube. We used 1,000 mm focus, 50 mm diameter.

1 Ask an adult to cut the plastic tubing to 39 in (1 m)—this is the focal length of the objective lens. Smooth the ends of the tube with sandpaper.

2 Remove the tops from the coupling and the reducer, and take out the rubber bands that you find inside. You may need an adult to help.

3 Measure the diameter of the reducer. Draw a circle of the same diameter on thick, black cardboard, and cut it out.

Viewfinder

4 Cut out the center of the cardboard circle. This is your viewfinder. Fit it into the top of the reducer.

5 Put the top of the reducer, fitted with the viewfinder, back onto the body of the reducer.

6 Put the eyepiece lens into the end of the coupling. Fix the lens with plastic putty or glue.

7 Slot the reducer into the coupling. It must slide in and out smoothly. This is the eyepiece of the telescope.

8 Now place the objective lens into the top of the coupling and secure it firmly with plastic putty.

9 Use plastic putty to fix the lens and the top of the coupling onto the end of the telescope tube. Slot the eyepiece into the other end of the telescope.

Eyepiece lens

Objective lens

Telescope tube

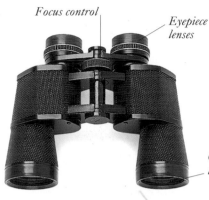

Types of telescopes
There are several types of optical telescopes. Reflectors use lenses and curved mirrors to collect light. Refractors use only lenses. Both kinds can be used by amateur astronomers.

What to buy

It is often easier to begin scanning the sky with a good pair of binoculars. They are more portable, and they generally give a higher quality image than telescopes in the same price range. With binoculars, you'll see about ten times more than with the naked eye. You'll see even more with a telescope, but wait until you know your way around the sky before you move on—it can be confusing to see too much at once.

Focus control

Eyepiece lenses

Objective lens

Basic refractor telescopes like this one are popular with amateur astronomers.

Finder scope

Eyepiece lens magnifies image.

Focusing knob

The diameter of the main lens dictates how much light enters the telescope.

Use a stand to support your telescope steadily.

Mount

Binoculars

Binoculars are in fact two telescopes joined together. This gives them a wide viewing range, showing brilliant star fields. Binoculars are stamped with numbers, such as 7 x 50. The first figure is the number of times a distant object will seem closer; the second is the diameter of the objective lens.

Telescopes

If you decide to buy a telescope, think carefully about the work you want it to do. Different types of telescopes are used for different jobs. Cost and size are other points to consider. Look around to find out what's available.

What you can see

You may see craters with your naked eye.

Naked eye
You can pick out dark "seas" (plains) on the Moon.

Binoculars
With standard binoculars, you will be able to see most of the larger craters on the Moon, especially those found on the shadow boundary between the lit and dark areas. Mountain ranges also become visible.

Telescopes
You should see the finest details of the major craters, in addition to shadows crossing the mountain ranges. You may pick out variations in the color of the dark seas. By looking for slight changes over time, amateurs can add to our knowledge of the Moon.

10 Decorate your telescope with stickers or spray paint. Practice using a small telescope to help when you move on to bigger instruments.

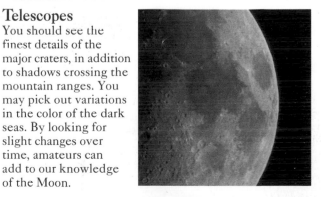

The solar system

Planetarium
This 19th-century device was used to show how the planets move around the Sun.

Earth's closest neighbors are the planets, moons, comets, and rocks that orbit our star, the Sun. Together, this family makes up the solar system. The Sun and planets formed about 4.6 billion years ago, from a whirling disk of gas and dust. The Sun formed first, with the planets and other bodies created from the material that was left over. The planets are not alike, although they are of two main types: the inner rocky planets—Mercury, Venus, Earth, and Mars—and the "gas giants"—Jupiter, Saturn, Uranus, and Neptune. Tiny, icy Pluto doesn't fit into either group, and some astronomers have suggested that it is a moon that escaped from Neptune. However, Pluto is so distant that we know very little about it.

Make a solar system
The inner, rocky planets with their rigid surfaces are very different than the gas giants. At first, the gaseous planets were only a little bigger than the rocky worlds. However, this gave them a stronger gravitational pull, so they attracted extra gas from the Sun and grew much bigger than the rocky planets. Learn more about the planets by making this model.

You will need
- balloon
- newspaper strips
- flour-and-water paste
- cotton batting
- red and yellow tissue
- tray, lined with foil
- plant spray • glue
- *either* balls of various sizes *or* modeling clay
- thin cardboard
- compasses
- paints and brushes
- swizzle sticks or dowels
- cardboard base

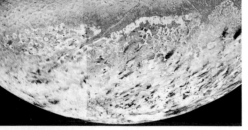

Try molding the planets yourself from modeling clay.

6 Using the approximate scale on page 15, either buy balls of the right size or make them from clay. These will be the planets.

7 Use watercolors to paint each of the planets, using the model below as your guide to their different colors.

Smaller bodies
Beside the planets, there are much smaller objects in the solar system, including over 60 satellites (moons), countless comets, and hundreds of thousands of asteroids.

Satellites
Aside from Mercury and Venus, all the planets have satellites. Saturn has the most, with 18. The easiest ones to see are the four largest moons of Jupiter, which you can spot with binoculars or a telescope. With a big telescope you can see some of Saturn's moons too.

Asteroids
There are asteroid belts between Mars and Jupiter, and beyond Pluto. Asteroids are hard to spot but you may observe some of the brightest with a telescope.

Solar system facts
- The Sun is so much more massive than the rest of the solar system put together that the pull of its gravity holds the planets in orbit.
- The giant gas worlds are mostly formed of rapidly spinning hydrogen gas, with ammonia and methane mixed in.
- Mars is the planet most similar to Earth, but it cannot support life as we know it.

Each planet spins on its own axis while orbiting the Sun.

Pluto

Neptune

Saturn

Uranus

Jupiter

Venus

Earth

Mercury

Mars

The Sun is almost 93 million miles (150 million km) away from Earth.

SUN

Planet orbits
The time a planet takes to travel around the Sun is its year. These vary, depending on the planet's distance from the Sun; for example, Pluto takes 248.6 Earth years to orbit the Sun.

Flour-and-water paste

Put the tissue in a foil-lined tray.

1 Blow up a balloon to the size of a soccer ball. This will be the Sun. Paste strips of newspaper all over it.

2 Paste layers of paper on the balloon to build up a coat of papier-mâché. When it is dry, paint the surface yellow.

3 Place cotton batting onto red and yellow tissue paper and wet it all well. The dyes will soak into the cotton batting.

4 Use a water-based glue to stick the cotton batting onto the Sun. This gives the Sun a textured appearance.

5 Flick fine specks of red paint onto the finished Sun. (Cover the tabletop to protect the surrounding area.)

Make sure the inner circle is wider than its planet.

8 Make rings for the gas planets by measuring two circles onto cardboard, one inside the other.

9 Color and cut out the rings. Use small swizzle sticks to support the rings, and push them through the planets.

10 Balance the paper rings around each ringed planet. Make sure the rings are tilted at an angle, as below.

11 Now fix all the planets to swizzle sticks or dowel rods. Fix them securely with either glue or putty.

12 Attach the planets to a large cardboard base, in the correct sequence outward from the Sun.

The finished model

The finished model shows the order of the planets from the Sun, but not the immense scale of distances. To do this, if Mercury were 4 in (10 cm) from the Sun, Pluto would need to be 32 ft (10 m) away!

Model planets, approx. sizes	
Mercury	0.8 in (2 mm)
Venus	0.3 in (7 mm)
Earth	0.3 in (7mm)
Mars	0.1 in (3 mm)
Jupiter	3.0 in (72 mm)
Saturn	2.0 in (60 mm)
Uranus	1.0 in (22 mm)
Neptune	1.0 in (22 mm)
Pluto	0.8 in (2 mm)

Blue-green Earth is the only planet with plentiful water on its surface.

Saturn's rings are over 167,800 miles (270,000 km) in diameter.

The rings of the gas planets tilt at different angles.

MERCURY   VENUS   EARTH   MARS   JUPITER   SATURN   URANUS   NEPTUNE   PLUTO

Planet projects

The easiest planets to see are Venus, Mars, Jupiter, and Saturn. They look like bright stars but, when you view them through binoculars or a telescope, you will see that they are tiny disks of light rather than twinkly pinpoints, like the stars. However, you would need quite a large telescope to see much surface detail. As a long-term project, once you have located the planets, you should record their movement by watching them over a period of a few weeks. Don't try to observe Mercury, it is dangerously close to the Sun. Neptune, Uranus, and Pluto are too faint and distant for a new astronomer to spot.

Phases of Venus

Venus is visible just before sunrise or just after sunset, when it looks like the brightest star in the sky. Like the Moon, Venus goes through phases, changing from a full to a crescent shape. You can follow these with a telescope, and will see the planet change in apparent size, depending on its distance from Earth. The surface of Venus is permanently hidden by a dense layer of cloud.

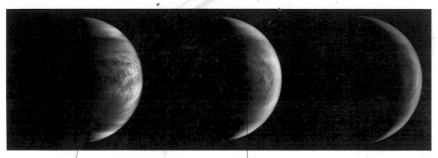

Venus is sometimes known as the morning star or the evening star.

Venus's surface is covered by a thick atmosphere of carbon dioxide.

Jupiter

Vast Jupiter reflects a lot of sunlight, which makes it easy to spot from Earth. Looking through a small telescope, you'll see that the gassy giant looks squashed at top and bottom and bulges at the equator. This is caused by centrifugal force, the result of the planet's surprisingly rapid rotation – Jupiter spins around in slightly less than ten hours. Try this experiment to see why Jupiter bulges as it spins.

You will need

- thin, red cardboard
- yellow and red paper
- paint and brushes
- wooden rod
- scissors • compasses

1 Cut a length of wooden rod so it measures 15 in (38 cm). Paint it a bright color.

2 Cut two circles from red cardboard, 1¼ in (3 cm) and 1½ in (4 cm) across. Cut a third circle, also 1½ in (4 cm) across, from red paper.

Jupiter's rapid spin forms the planet's gassy surface into belts and zones.

3 On a cutting board, make small cuts in the center of each circle, so they can slip onto the wooden rod. Check that the disks fit. Put them to one side.

Bubbles and spots, some bigger than Earth, swirl on Jupiter's surface.

Mars's rusty surface

From Earth, Mars looks like a reddish disk. Its color is due to iron compounds that have rusted in the soil. Rust cannot be formed without water and oxygen, as well as iron, so apparently there was once water on Mars.

You will need

- iron filings
- paper towels
- water spritzer
- small plastic tray.

Dust storms on Mars sometimes blot its surface features from our view.

1 Line a plastic tray with a paper towel and dampen it well with a water spritzer.

The simulated surface of Mars

2 Sprinkle the iron filings very finely over the damp paper. Put the tray to one side.

3 For the next few days, keep the filings slightly damp, though not too wet or too dry.

4 The iron eventually turns rusty red, just as once happened on Mars

Each strip of paper should measure ½ x 12 in (1 x 30 cm).

4 Stick strips of yellow paper onto a piece of red cardboard measuring 4 x 12 in (8 x 30 cm). Cut the paper into eight strips.

Remember that the strips of paper should be evenly spaced.

5 Stick the paper strips around the 1½-in (4-cm) cardboard circle. Make sure that the strips are spaced regularly around the disk.

6 Glue the paper circle 7 in (18 cm) from the top of the rod—about halfway down. Glue the circle with the paper attached 1¼ in (3 cm) from the top.

7 Slide the remaining cardboard disk onto the bottom of the rod. It should fit fairly loosely. Then curve the bottom of each strip of paper around, and attach it to this disk.

Jupiter watch

Bright Jupiter moves slowly against the stars, and takes about a year to move through each of the zodiac constellations (see page 28).

8 Spin the model and watch "Jupiter" bulge. The real planet is not a perfect sphere; it is fatter in the middle than around the poles.

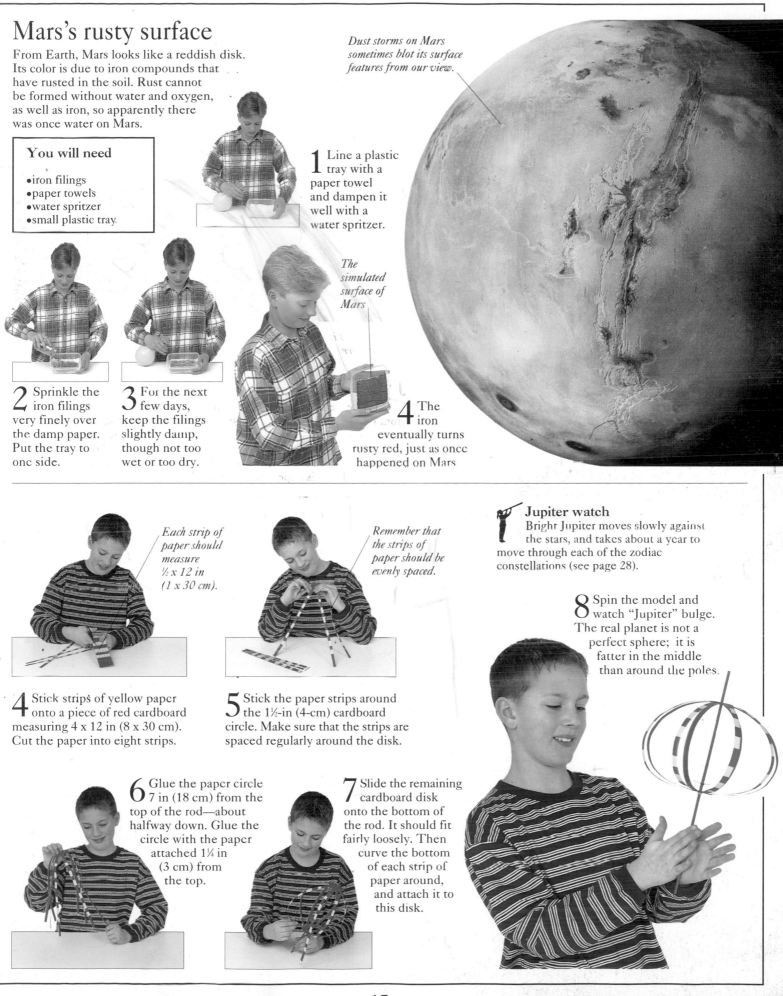

Looking at the Moon

The Moon is one of the easiest objects for an astronomer to study. At 238,906 miles (384,400 km) away, you can pick out many features with the naked eye, while binoculars or a telescope reveal even more detail. The dark areas are known as seas, because this is what astronomers once believed them to be. In fact, they are lowland plains of dark lava. The brighter areas are highlands. The surface is heavily cratered, and a small telescope reveals many mountain ranges.

The Terminator
You can see the craters on the Moon's surface most clearly when they are on the Terminator, the boundary line between the dark and the sunlit half.

The Apennines are the highest mountains on the Moon.

The seas on the Moon are also known as maria, from the Latin word mare, *for sea.*

The Alps are the most spectacular mountains on the Moon. Look for them close to the dark crater, Plato.

MARE FRIGORIS
Sea of Cold

Plato

Alps Mtns

Caucasus Mtns

MARE IMBRIUM
Sea of Rains

MARE SERENITATIS
Sea of Serenity

MARE CRISIUM
Sea of Crises

Apennine Mtns

MARE TRANQUILLITATIS
Sea of Tranquillity

MARE VAPORUM
Sea of Vapours

▲ Apollo 11

MARE FECUNDITATIS
Sea of Fertility

Aristarchus

Copernicus

Pyrenees Mtns

MARE PROCELLARUM
Ocean of Storms

Kepler

Ptolomaeus

MARE NECTARIS
Sea of Nectar

MARE NUBIUM
Sea of Clouds

MARE HUMORUM
Sea of Moisture

Tycho

Look out for ...
• The long shadows across craters and mountains, which change nightly.
• Large seas, such as the Sea of Crises, that can be seen with the naked eye.
• The bright rays extending from the ray-crater Tycho, which extend for hundreds of miles but can only be seen when the Moon is full or almost full.

The far side
The first people to see the far side of the Moon were astronauts, because it always keeps the same side turned away from Earth. The far side is mostly cratered, but there is one dark sea, called Tsiolkovsky.

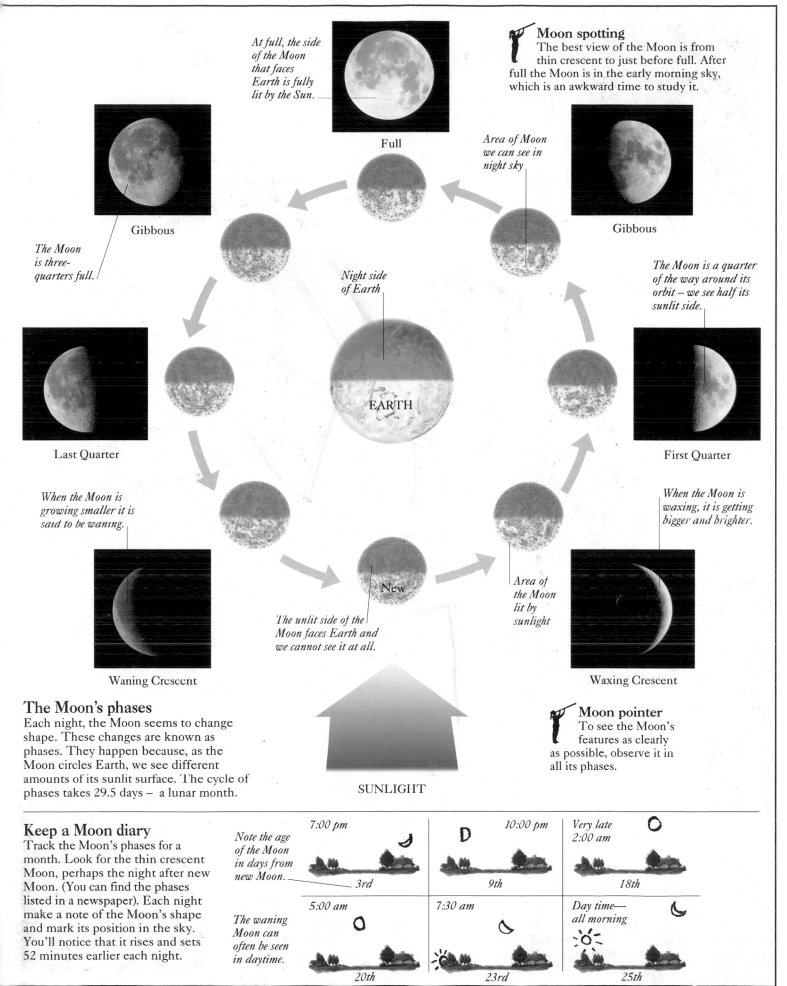

At full, the side
of the Moon
that faces
Earth is fully
lit by the Sun.

Full

Area of Moon
we can see in
night sky

Moon spotting
The best view of the Moon is from
thin crescent to just before full. After
full the Moon is in the early morning sky,
which is an awkward time to study it.

Gibbous

*The Moon
is three-
quarters full.*

Gibbous

*The Moon is a quarter
of the way around its
orbit – we see half its
sunlit side.*

*Night side
of Earth*

EARTH

Last Quarter

First Quarter

*When the Moon is
growing smaller it is
said to be waning.*

*When the Moon is
waxing, it is getting
bigger and brighter.*

New

*Area of
the Moon
lit by
sunlight*

*The unlit side of the
Moon faces Earth and
we cannot see it at all.*

Waning Crescent

Waxing Crescent

The Moon's phases
Each night, the Moon seems to change
shape. These changes are known as
phases. They happen because, as the
Moon circles Earth, we see different
amounts of its sunlit surface. The cycle of
phases takes 29.5 days – a lunar month.

SUNLIGHT

Moon pointer
To see the Moon's
features as clearly
as possible, observe it in
all its phases.

Keep a Moon diary
Track the Moon's phases for a
month. Look for the thin crescent
Moon, perhaps the night after new
Moon. (You can find the phases
listed in a newspaper). Each night
make a note of the Moon's shape
and mark its position in the sky.
You'll notice that it rises and sets
52 minutes earlier each night.

*Note the age
of the Moon
in days from
new Moon.*

7:00 pm

3rd

10:00 pm

9th

Very late
2:00 am

18th

*The waning
Moon can
often be seen
in daytime.*

5:00 am

20th

7:30 am

23rd

Day time—
all morning

25th

Lunar eclipses

The Moon is the brightest object in the sky, but sometimes this brightness is dramatically dimmed, when the full Moon is slowly covered by Earth's shadow. This is called a lunar eclipse. The Moon does not vanish, but appears to be a dull coppery-red color. Eclipses only happen when the Sun, full Moon, and Earth are completely aligned, so that the Earth blocks the Sun's light and casts a shadow on the Moon.

Red Moon

The reddish color of the Moon during an eclipse is caused by Earth's atmosphere. Although Earth blocks the Moon from the Sun, the atmosphere bends a little sunlight to light the Moon. However, only red rays of light survive the journey; these give the Moon a coppery tinge.

Make a lunar eclipse

Build a model of Earth and the Moon in space, with a flashlight to represent the Sun. Then dim the lights, so that your room becomes a laboratory, where you can cast the shadow of Earth onto the Moon, and so stage your own lunar eclipse.

You will need
- baseboard
- flashlight • dowels
- globes for the Earth and the Moon
- paints • scissors
- glue or plastic putty

1 Find a modeling ball 2 in (5 cm) in diameter to represent the Earth, and a modeling ball 1 in (2.5 cm) in diameter for the Moon. Paint Earth blue and green, and the Moon gray.

Paint the dowels a dark color.

2 Cut two lengths of dowels, about 7 in (18 cm) to support the Earth and 7½ in (19 cm) for the Moon. Glue the balls securely onto the rods, or stick them on with plastic putty.

The baseboard and rods should be dark so they do not reflect the light.

3 Cut a rectangle of dark cardboard to make a base, measuring 16½ x 6 in (42 x 15 cm). Cut two holes in the center of the board, 12 in (30 cm) apart. Push in Earth and glue it securely into place.

4 Glue the Moon into the baseboard opposite the larger Earth. It's important to check that the centers of both globes are level with each other. If you need to, adjust the height of the supporting dowels.

5 Hold your flashlight level with the Earth-Moon model. When the Sun's light falls fully on the Moon as well as Earth, the Moon is brightly lit in the night sky.

6 Pivot the board so that the Moon, Earth, and Sun are totally aligned. Earth blocks the Sun's light, leaving the Moon in shadow—a total eclipse.

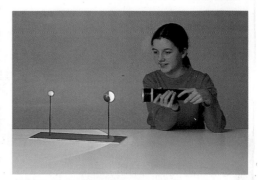

7 Pivot the board again, so that only part of Earth's shadow falls on the Moon. This is when we see a partial lunar eclipse. The effect is less noticeable.

The surface of the Moon

There is no water on the Moon and it has no atmosphere, so it cannot support life. Without an atmosphere, there is no weather, so the surface rocks have not been eroded by the effects of rain or wind, or worn away by the tides. The surface is covered in loose, fine-grained soil.

Bumpy surface

There are hundreds of thousands of craters on the Moon—about 500,000 of them are 4,920 ft (1,500 m) across. Many of them are rimmed by mountain ranges, which can form walls around the craters thousands of feet high.

Moon rock

Moon rocks can be seen in museums. The main types are basalt, a kind of volcanic rock, and breccia, made of soil and pieces of rock squeezed together by the impact of falling objects.

Astronauts

Scientists have been able to study Moon rocks because the Apollo astronauts brought samples back to Earth.

Make a lunar landscape

As you can see through your binoculars, the surface of the Moon is pitted with craters of all sizes. These were caused by meteorites, constantly bombarding the Moon soon after it formed. The fragments of rock hit the Moon at high speed and exploded, creating circular craters many times their own size. Try making craters for yourself.

You will need

•pebbles •foil •tray
•plaster of Paris •water
•bowl •paper •spoon

Craters

The impact of the missiles on the plaster before it hardens creates a cratered surface, just like the one on the Moon.

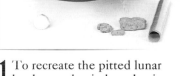

1 To recreate the pitted lunar landscape, begin by selecting some pebble "meteorites," wrapped in foil to make them round.

Line a tray with cooking foil, so that the plaster does not stick to the tray.

2 Empty plaster of Paris into a foil-lined tray and spread it evenly over the bottom. Then level the surface of the plaster.

Stir the plaster all the time.

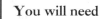

3 Gradually pour water from a jug into the powder. Be quick, so that the plaster does not set before you are ready. If it is thin, add more powder.

4 Wait for the plaster to thicken, but not set. Then drop missiles from chest height into the tray, as often as possible.

Newspaper protects the floor from splatters.

The Sun

Corona
The outermost layer of the Sun, the corona, can be seen during a total eclipse.

Solar eclipses
One of the most dramatic sights in the sky is a total solar eclipse, when the Sun seems to vanish. Eclipses happen when the Moon comes between us and the Sun, briefly hiding the Sun and casting a shadow on Earth. The eclipse can only be seen by places covered by the shadow, which is less than 160 miles wide.

Of all the stars in the sky, the nearest to us is the Sun. A glowing ball of gas, it is so large that Earth could fit inside it one million times. Surface temperatures reach 11,000°F, rising to 27 million°F at the center. Despite these amazing facts, the Sun is an ordinary star. It only seems big and bright compared with other stars because it is so much closer. By studying the Sun, astronomers have learned a lot about the stars. But never forget that the Sun's light is very dangerous.

DANGER!
NEVER LOOK STRAIGHT AT THE SUN

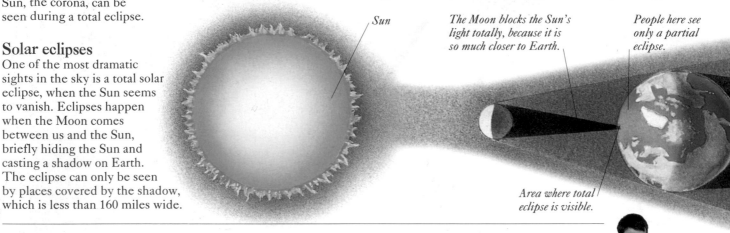

Sun

The Moon blocks the Sun's light totally, because it is so much closer to Earth.

People here see only a partial eclipse.

Area where total eclipse is visible.

Observing the Sun

Looking directly at the Sun through binoculars, a telescope, or with your eyes alone is VERY dangerous. There is only one safe way to observe the Sun – by projecting its image onto cardboard.

You will need

- ruler • compasses • binoculars
- stiff cardboard • plastic putty
- craft knife • white cardboard

Use a pair of compasses to draw the circles.

Eyepiece end of binoculars

1 Measure one of the front (eyepiece) ends of your binoculars.

2 On a piece of cardboard, draw a circle half the width of the eyepiece end.

3 Using a craft knife (with adult help if you need it) cut out the circle; be careful!

4 Match the cut-out circle to one of the lenses. Then use plastic putty to stick the binoculars to the cardboard.

Sunlight

5 Make a screen from white cardboard, to receive the Sun's reflection. Hold the binoculars about 3 ft (1 m) from the cardboard, so that their shadow falls on the stand. Turn the binoculars until the disk of the Sun is seen on the screen. Focus them until the image of the Sun is sharp.

Sun's image

The Sun's heat

About half the Sun's energy comes out as light, and half as heat. Demonstrate the heat of the Sun by following this simple experiment—ask an adult's permission first.

You will need

- magnifying glass
- bar of chocolate
- plate

Be careful to focus the sunlight onto the chocolate, not any nearby surfaces.

Prominences can stretch for tens of thousands of miles. Some last for hours, others for months.

The Sun's blotchy appearance is caused by hot gases rising to its surface.

1 Focus sunlight through a magnifying glass onto a bar of chocolate. The chocolate melts very quickly. This heat energy is only a tiny part of the powerful radiation that comes from the Sun.

Powerhouse

Like other stars, the Sun is a ball of gas. At its core, violent nuclear reactions constantly take place. These generate energy that spreads out as light, heat, and other radiation. Without energy from the Sun, life could not exist on Earth. The Sun fuses four million tons of hydrogen every second, and has enough hydrogen to keep going for five billion years.

Mapping sunspots

Once you have projected the Sun's image onto cardboard, you should be able to map the sunspots that cross its surface. These are darker, cooler areas on the face of the Sun. A typical sunspot is tens of thousands of miles across. They develop in hours, but can last for months.

You will need

- projection screen
- tracing paper
- tape
- pencil or pen

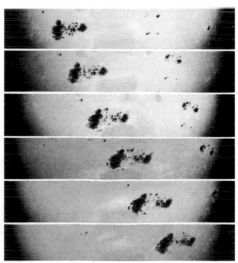

Sunspot cycle
There is a cycle of activity in sunspots, reaching a peak every 11 years. Sometimes there are no sunspots at all.

1 To record sunspots, tape a piece of tracing paper over the projection screen. Draw a circle around the disk of the Sun and mark the position of any dark spots with a pencil. Over time, this shows how the spots change.

2 Observations or photos of the Sun over time show that the spots are in a different place from day to day. Using sunspots as markers proves that the Sun takes 28 days to rotate.

The Earth in space

The position of our planet in space affects life on Earth. For example, Earth is covered in water only because it is the right temperature: close to the Sun, but not too close. Earth is just the right size, so its gravity holds the atmosphere that we breathe, which means the oceans do not evaporate. We are also affected by the position of our neighbor the Moon, which is large enough for its gravitational pull to influence Earth's oceans, causing the tides.

The Earth and the Moon
In this photo, taken by the Apollo astronauts, the Moon's barren surface contrasts with the blue-green, watery Earth.

The pull of gravity

Gravity is the force of attraction felt between two bodies. Earth's gravity controls the Moon in orbit, while the Moon's gravity pulls up the tides in Earth's oceans. This experiment uses magnetism to show how gravity pulls objects toward each other. Magnetism is not gravity, but the effect is similar.

1 Use a craft knife to cut an L-shaped arm from foamboard at least 1 in (2 cm) deep. The arm should be 8½ in (22 cm) tall and 6 in (15 cm) across the top.

You will need

- thick foamboard •craft knife
- ruler •pen •cardboard •thread
- four magnets •glue or plastic putty

The stand must be sturdy enough to support the weight of a swinging magnet.

2 Now make a base from thick cardboard, measuring about 8½ x 5 in (22 x 12 cm). Cover the base and the suspension arm with colored paper.

3 Fix the arm to the cardboard base securely, using glue or plastic putty. Tie a piece of thread about 10 in (25 cm) long to the upright arm.

The magnets attract and repel one another.

6 Set the free magnet swinging and watch the path it follows, depending on how close it is to the fixed magnets. The fixed magnets attract the free magnet. This mimics gravity.

4 Tie a magnet on the end of the thread. It should be suspended about 1 in (2.5 cm) above the base, and be able to swing freely.

5 Fix three magnets loosely onto the baseboard, using plastic putty. The fixed magnets can be arranged in patterns to attract the swinging magnet.

Mapping the stars

From Earth, the stars seem to be studded across the inside of a vast sphere. Although we know that this isn't true, astronomers find it helpful to picture a celestial sphere when they want to map the stars. Just as geographers map the Earth's surface by referring to imaginary lines of latitude and longitude, astronomers plot the positions of the stars, Sun, and Moon by referring to lines of celestial longitude (Declination) and latitude (Right Ascension). These are marked on many star charts.

Stars arranged into imaginary shapes

A changing view
Our view of the stars changes as the Earth spins on its axis, and also as it orbits the Sun. At any time of year, we see different parts of the celestial sphere.

Earth inside the "celestial sphere"

Line of Declination

Across and along
Lines of Declination (Dec.) run in rings parallel with the equator. Lines of Right Ascension (RA) run through the celestial poles. Declination is expressed in degrees (°) and Right Ascension in hours and minutes.

Line of Right Ascension

North and south
An imaginary line, the equator, divides the Earth into two halves, or hemispheres. People who live in the southern hemisphere see mostly different stars than people who live in the northern hemisphere.

Seasons

The Earth is tilted on its axis. This means that during its orbit around the Sun, different levels of sunlight reach places on Earth at different times, causing the changing seasons. This activity shows how the lengths of day and night change with the seasons, too: days are shorter in winter than in summer.

The South pole points toward the Sun during summer in the southern hemisphere.

You will need:
- lamp ("the Sun")
- globe
- books or boxes

1 Make sure the top of the globe is level with the "Sun" lamp. The southern hemisphere should be pointed toward the Sun—this is summer.

2 Switch the lamp on and turn Earth through one day. The southern hemisphere gets daylight for longer than the north. Now try the experiment with the north in the summer position.

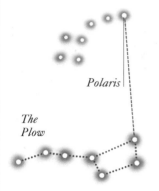

Polaris

The Plow

Northern hemisphere

Ancient astronomers found their way around the skies by dividing the stars into patterns, or constellations. We still use these constellations, which generally take the form of people, animals, or birds. You can't see all of them at once; only part of the sky can be seen from a particular spot on the Earth's surface at one time. The map on this page shows the stars visible in the northern hemisphere through the year.

Finding Polaris
Polaris, the North or Pole Star, is the only star that seems to stay in the same place as the Earth spins. Find it by extending a line through the "pointer stars" in the Plow, also called Ursa Major, the Great Bear.

Take your time
At first, it will be easier to find stars on the map than in the sky. But with practice, you will soon recognize the star patterns.

Stars near the center of the map can be seen year-round.

Star chart constellations and months:

JUNE · JULY · AUGUST · SEPTEMBER · OCTOBER · NOVEMBER · DECEMBER · JANUARY · FEBRUARY · MARCH · APRIL · MAY

LUPUS · SCORPIUS · CORONA AUSTRALIS · SAGITTARIUS · LIBRA · SERPENS CAPUT · OPHIUCHUS · SERPENS CAUDA · AQUILA · CAPRICORNUS · CENTAURUS · VIRGO · HERCULES · LYRA · Vega · DELPHINUS · AQUARIUS · Arcturus · CORONA BOREALIS · DRACO · CYGNUS · PISCES AUSTRINUS · BOÖTES · Milky Way · PEGASUS · PISCES · CORVUS · URSA MAJOR · CEPHEUS · ANDROMEDA · CRATER · LEO MINOR · URSA MINOR · Polaris · CASSIOPEIA · SCULPTOR · HYDRA · LEO · SEXTANS · CANCER · LYNX · AURIGA · Capella · PERSEUS · ARIES · CETUS · PHOENIX · ANTLIA · VELA · GEMINI · TAURUS · CANIS MINOR · ORION · Rigel · ERIDANUS · FORNAX · MONOCEROS · PUPPIS · CANIS MAJOR · Sirius · LEPUS · CAELUM · COLUMBA

How to use this map
Find the current month at the edge of the map and turn the book until this month is at the bottom. Face south at night and look for the stars as they appear on the map. You should see most of the stars that appear in the center and lower part of the star chart.

In winter, the constellation of Orion is high in northern skies. Use it as a signpost to find your way around the heavens.

26

Make a quadrant

For centuries, sailors have used the stars to navigate. Early sailors used a device called a quadrant to find their direction. In the northern hemisphere, they measured the angle between the horizon and the Pole Star, Polaris. Because they knew that the altitude (height in degrees) of the Pole Star from any place on Earth is the same as that place's latitude, the sailors could tell where on Earth they were. Follow these instructions to make a quadrant of your own.

You will need
•compass •pencil •cardboard
•craft knife •thread •small bead
•felt-tipped pen •glue •ruler
•protractor •paper clip

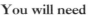
Southern pole
There is no polar star in the southern hemisphere. Polynesian sailors used the Southern Cross, which surrounds the polar point, to navigate.

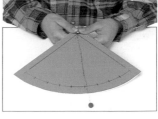

1 With compasses set 8 in (20 cm) apart, draw a quadrant (quarter circle) onto cardboard. Cut this out. Then mark lines 6 in (15 cm) long on the quadrant, ⅝ in (1.5 cm) from each straight edge.

2 Use compasses to draw an arc that links the straight lines. With a protractor and ruler, mark off degree divisions from 0° to 90°.

3 Tie a bead onto a piece of thread 10 in (25 cm) long. Tie the other end of the thread around a paper clip.

4 Push the paper clip through the axis point of your quadrant, and fold out the back of the clip.

Polaris
The Plow

Altitude
Altitude is measured from the equator, (which is 0°) to the polar point, (which is 90°). The altitude of the Pole Star from Sagres, Portugal is 37°, so Sagres's latitude is 37° north of the equator.

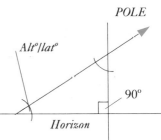
POLE
Alt°/lat°
90°
Horizon

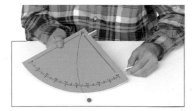

5 Trace two viewfinders, about 1 in (2.5 cm) high, onto stiff cardboard. Cut them out. Punch holes big enough to see through in the center.

The slot on the viewfinders must be the same width as the cardboard the quadrant is made from.

The reading is 37°.

Do not use the quadrant to look at the Sun.

Horizon

6 Slot the two viewfinders 1 in (2.5 cm) from the top and bottom of the quadrant. If necessary, glue them firmly.

Read off the angle here, where the string crosses the scale. This figure tells you the latitude you are on.

7 To make it easier to hold your quadrant, glue a block of cardboard to the back. It should be long and thick enough for your fingers to grip.

8 To use the quadrant, hold it up and squint at the polar star along the holes in the viewfinders. When the star is in line with both sight holes, take a reading on the scale. Steady the thread with a finger.

Southern hemisphere

Astronomers in the southern hemisphere look toward the center of the Milky Way, which contains the most stars in the galaxy. This is why the skies of the southern hemisphere are brighter and more beautiful than those in the north. The map opposite shows the stars visible in the south throughout the year.

You will need

- compasses • pencil • polyboard
- ping-pong ball • wooden stick
- paper • paints and brushes
- tape • flashlight bulb
- wires and clips • battery pack

The zodiacal band

Whether you are in the north or the south, you can see twelve constellations that are especially important. These form the background to the path the Sun, Moon, and planets seem to follow in the sky, and are called the zodiac constellations. As the Earth moves around the Sun during the year, this starry background changes as the Sun's bright light blocks our view of certain stars. Follow this experiment to understand how our perspective changes.

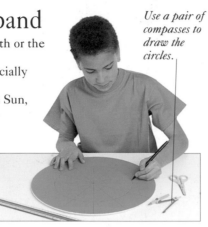

Use a pair of compasses to draw the circles.

1 Draw two circles on polyboard, one inside the other: 20 in (50 cm) and 31½ in (80 cm) across. Cut out the larger circle, and divide it into 12 equally sized pie sections. Label these counterclockwise with the months.

2 Paint a ping-pong ball to resemble Earth. Push a cocktail stick through the ball and support it with board, cut at 23° from the vertical. This is the angle at which Earth tilts.

Support the tilted Earth on a piece of board.

3 Copy the artwork below onto a sheet of paper 31½ x 4 in (80 x 10 cm). Join the ends of the paper and place this over the large, board base. Connect a flashlight bulb to a battery to represent the Sun.

4 With the Sun in the middle, move the Earth through the months. As it moves, you can see why the zodiac stars would not be visible against the real Sun—the Sun's light would blot them out.

See how the Sun seems to travel through the zodiac constellations as the Earth moves.

Keep the Earth pointing the same way.

Orion nebula
Learn to recognize the zodiac constellations as helpful pointers around the sky. The Orion nebula, shown above, in the constellation of Orion, is close to Taurus and Gemini.

In this artwork, the red line shows the path that the Sun seems to follow against the stars; the Moon and planets keep within the black lines.

April	March	February	January	December	November	October

PISCES	AQUARIUS	CAPRICORNUS	SAGITTARIUS	SCORPIUS	LIBRA

Stars of the southern skies

Light pollution is less of a problem in
the southern hemisphere, because
there are fewer land areas, and so fewer
people and street lights to dim the
stars. Look out for Sirius, the brightest
star, which lies in the constellation
Canis Major, the Great Dog.

*Stars near the celestial equator
can be seen from both
hemispheres; circumpolar
stars cannot be seen
outside their own
hemisphere.*

Crux (Southern Cross)

There is no single polar star in the south.
The constellation Crux (the Southern
Cross) is very close to the polar point.
Polynesian peoples used Crux to
navigate the Pacfic.

*The Southern
Cross is seen
here above the
clouds near the
Indian Ocean.*

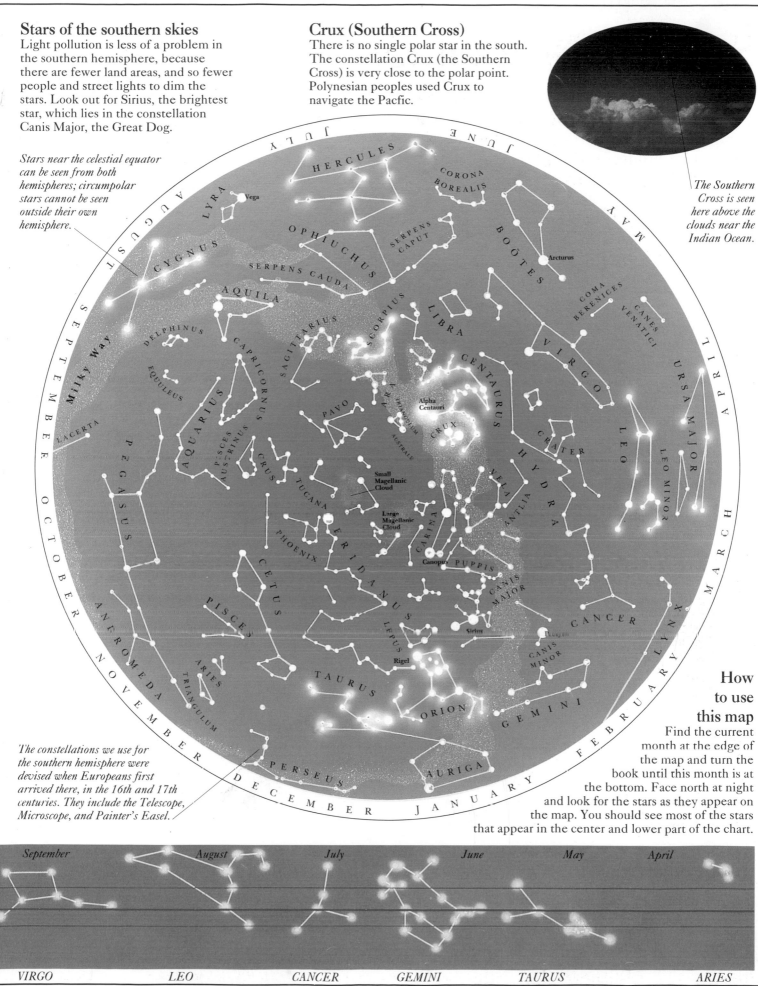

*The constellations we use for
the southern hemisphere were
devised when Europeans first
arrived there, in the 16th and 17th
centuries. They include the Telescope,
Microscope, and Painter's Easel.*

How to use this map

Find the current
month at the edge of
the map and turn the
book until this month is at
the bottom. Face north at night
and look for the stars as they appear on
the map. You should see most of the stars
that appear in the center and lower part of the chart.

September | August | July | June | May | April

VIRGO | LEO | CANCER | GEMINI | TAURUS | ARIES

Star light, star bright!

The stars appear at different levels of brightness. They are all so distant that they seem far fainter than our Sun, but of course many are far more luminous. Some relatively dim stars seem brighter to us than other, more luminous, stars because they are many light-years closer. This is why astronomers have devised scales that describe the actual brightness in addition to the apparent brightness for every star.

| 6 | 5 | 4 | 3 | 2 | 1 |

Star scale
The magnitude (brightness) of a star is described according to a scale of numbers. The scale above shows the six grades of brightness applied to stars visible to the naked eye. Brighter stars have low numbers; for example, Sirius, the brightest star, has a magnitude of -1.46.

Make a constellation
The stars in a constellation each seem to be fixed at the same distance from Earth, because we see them against a flat sky. In reality, they can be millions of light-years apart from each other. See this for yourself, by making a 3-D "map" of the constellation Cygnus (the Swan).

You will need
- colored cardboard
- pencil and ruler
- pearl "star" beads
- wooden rods
- felt-tipped pen
- craft knife
- string

1 On a piece of colored cardboard, 12 in (30 cm) square, mark out a grid, 12 x 2.5 cm (1 in). Pierce five holes on the grid, just as shown above.

Copy this drawing.

2 To support the "star" beads, cut wooden rods 2, 4½, 5½, 6, and 7 in (5, 11.5, 14, 15, and 18 cm) long. Glue the beads on top.

3 Draw the imaginary outline of a swan around the five holes, following the shape in the picture. Cut out the swan very carefully.

4 Stick the rods into the holes: A = 2 in (5 cm); B = 5½ in (14 cm); C = 4½ in (11.5 cm); D = 7 in (18 cm); E = 6 in (15 cm).

Farthest star from Earth

Nearest star to Earth

Spotting Cygnus
Cygnus (the Swan) can be seen from July to November, most of the night. In the northern hemisphere it will be high overhead. In the southern hemisphere, it will appear on the northern horizon.

Deneb

Albireo

5 This is how your 3-D Cygnus should now look. The labels give the names of important stars.

6 Suspend the model from the ceiling by attaching threads to each corner. All the threads should be the same length, so that the model is level when you hang it up.

7 With the stars on rods of different lengths, relative to their distances from Earth, notice how the shape of a swan is only obvious if you are right underneath the model (the view as it seems from Earth). In other positions, you see a different shape. This shows that the constellations we see on Earth would look entirely different, viewed from elsewhere in space.

Double stars

Not all stars are single stars. Some of the dots of light we see on Earth are in fact two stars, in orbit around each other. Often one of the pair will be fainter. As they orbit each other, the fainter star may pass in front of the brighter one, eclipsing it and reducing its brightness. This is one reason why some stars vary in brightness over a few weeks. Make a model of an eclipsing double star to see how this happens.

You will need

- cutting board • craft knife
- paper • pencil
- tape • cardboard
- flashlight bulb
- bulb holder • batteries and battery-box connectors
- soft plastic bubble

Ask an adult to supervise when you use a craft knife.

1 Collect the materials you need. Cut a piece of paper 6 x 8 in (15 x 20 cm), and wrap it around a pencil. Tape the paper in place to make a hollow tube that supports your model.

2 From cardboard, cut an egg-shaped base about 3½ in (8 cm) long and 2½ in (6 cm) wide. Cut a small hole toward the left of the cardboard base and slot the paper tube tightly inside, fitting it firmly to the cardboard base.

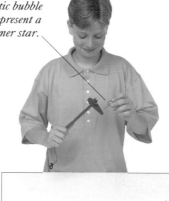

Color the plastic bubble to represent a dimmer star.

3 Run the battery-box connectors through the tube and connect them to the bulb holder, on top of the cardboard base. Screw in the bulb.

4 Fix the plastic bubble (the "dim star") to a rod and put it opposite the bright star bulb on the cardboard base. The bulbs' centers must be level.

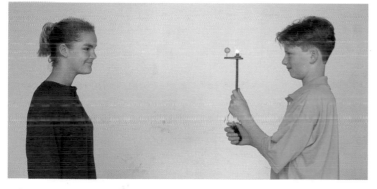

5 Connect the battery box so that the flashlight bulb lights up. In a darkened room, slowly rotate the tube. Watch as the dim star moves around its brighter companion, and note how the total light output changes. If you ask a friend to help with this, you can watch from a distance so that the two stars appear very close together.

6 When the stars are apart, the brighter light is undimmed. There is little light from the companion.

7 As the dim star moves in front of its brighter companion, the total light output drops suddenly.

8 The light from the dim star is much fainter than its companion. It will be hours before the light output rises.

Star colors

Stars are different colors, depending on their temperature. Red stars are the coolest, with a surface temperature of 6,300°F (3,500°C); blue stars are the hottest at 90,000°F (50,000°C). Our Sun is a mid-range, yellow star, with a temperature of 10,800°F (6,000°C). You can see these contrasting colors in the cluster of many-hued stars known as the Jewel Box, in the constellation of the Southern Cross, around the bright star Kappa.

Comets and meteors

Spotting comets or meteors can be thrilling for new astronomers, especially since their appearance is often unexpected. Every year, a handful of comets pass through the Earth's sky. These "dirty snowballs" are bodies of ice and rock, often in orbit at the very edge of the solar system. When a comet's orbit takes it closer to the Sun, it starts to thaw, releasing jets of glowing gases that we see as a bright tail. Many meteors come from the dust of comets. When these fragments of debris enter the Earth's atmosphere, they burn up in a streak of light—which is why they are sometimes known as shooting stars.

Comet watch
Use binoculars to look for comets on a moonless night. Often they are very faint and fuzzy, but they become brighter as they approach the Sun.

An icy heart
The frozen nucleus (center) of a comet is only a few miles across. As it heats up, the nucleus releases gases that surround it in a vast glowing cloud, called a coma. Comets sometimes have two tails: a broad, curved dust tail, and a thin, straight tail made of gas.

A comet's tail

The tail of a comet always points away from the Sun. This is due to the solar wind, a stream of energy particles that flows from the Sun in all directions. The wind pushes back the melted ice and gas from the comet's nucleus. As a result, when a comet is traveling away from the Sun, it looks as if it is going backward.

You will need
- modeling straw • ping-pong ball
- colored paper • scissors • tape
- cardboard • hair dryer

The rod should be firmly positioned in the center of the cardboard.

1 Cut a plastic modeling straw so it is 8 in (20 cm) long. This will be used to support your model comet.

2 From cardboard, cut out a base that measures 6 x 6 in (15 x 15 cm). Cover this with colored paper.

3 Cut a hole in the base big enough to provide a tight fit for the support rod. Glue the rod into the hole.

The strips should all hang in the same direction.

Predicting comets
Some comets orbit the Sun only once, and never return. Others come back regularly, such as Halley's Comet, which orbits the Sun every 76 years.

4 Cut 12 to 15 strips of colored tissue paper, 6 in (15 cm) long and ½ in (1 cm) wide. Using double-sided tape, fix the tissue around a ping-pong ball.

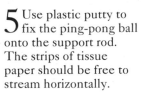

5 Use plastic putty to fix the ping-pong ball onto the support rod. The strips of tissue paper should be free to stream horizontally.

Meteor radiants

At certain times each year, the Earth passes through a stream of dust left by old comets. As a result, a meteor shower streaks across the sky. The meteors all seem to radiate from a single point in the sky, but in fact are traveling in parallel paths. Try this experiment to understand why the meteors seem to spread out.

You will need

- straws
- plastic putty
- shallow dish

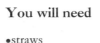

The straws represent meteor streaks.

1 Stick 12 to 24 straws into a dish lined with plasticine. Make sure they are all parallel to each other. Look straight down onto the straws.

2 The straws are parallel to each other but to your eye, they appear tilted over from the center of the plate. This is how a meteor shower appears to us.

Meteor watch

If you watch the skies on any clear, dark night, you will probably spot a meteor before long. They range in brightness from faint gleams to fireballs that look like a UFO and can light up the sky as brightly as the Moon.

Meteor showers

Meteor showers occur on the same dates each year. They take their name from the constellation in which their radiant lies, for example, the Orionids, found in Orion each October. So-called meteor storms are very heavy meteor showers. They are far more rare.

In this stony-iron meteorite, metal encloses the rock-filled material.

Meteorites

If a meteor is substantial enough to survive the journey through the atmosphere to land on the Earth, it is called a meteorite. Most are made of stone.

Shooting stars

Meteors flare up because they are traveling at many miles per second. The friction of the air at such speed burns them up and causes a trail of light. A particle the size of a grain of sand can become a bright meteor.

6 Turn a hair dryer on your comet and study what happens. You should find that the streamers representing the comet's tail blow out horizontally behind it. The airflow from the dryer represents the energy from the Sun, the solar wind.

Gravity
The pull of gravity is the force that keeps the stars, gas, and dust whirling around together in the form of galaxies.

Galaxies

The thousands of stars that crowd the night sky are only a few of the billions in our "star city," or galaxy. A galaxy is a massive grouping of stars, held together by gravity. We call our galaxy the Milky Way because from Earth its center resembles a ribbon of milky light across the sky. There may be trillions of galaxies in the Universe; you will be able to see some of them with your binoculars or telescope, visible as faint patches of hazy light. These objects are unimaginably distant from Earth. For example, the Andromeda galaxy, visible with the naked eye in the Andromeda constellation, is more than two million light-years away.

Make a spinning galaxy
The Milky Way is a spiral galaxy. Seen from space, a spiral galaxy looks like a rotating wheel of stars. At the massive hub, or center, are cooler, red stars; blue, hotter stars spin around in the great arms. The gas and dust from which new stars will form are found mainly in the arms as well. Follow these instructions to help you picture the structure of our own, and millions of other, galaxies.

You will need

- red and blue paper
- dark cardboard • ruler
- pair of compasses
- scissors
- wooden stick
- glue

Look for the Milky Way on a moonless night, away from city lights.

Milky Way
The Milky Way is brightest toward the center of the galaxy, which lies in the constellation Sagittarius. In places, such as the Coalsack near the Southern Cross, clouds of space dust dim the light from the center of the galaxy.

1 Trace a swirling spiral shape onto a circle of blue paper, 4½ in (12 cm) across. Trace a similar, smaller spiral onto a red paper circle. Cut both shapes out.

3 Glue the blue spiral shape onto the center of the cardboard circle. Then stick the red paper spiral on top.

Use a water-based glue.

Groups of stars

Stars are often found in close groups or clusters, held together by gravity. Sometimes this is because they were formed at the same time from a mass of gas and dust. These clusters mostly form at opposite ends of a star's life.

The bright stars in the Pleiades are also known as the Seven Sisters.

Open clusters
Open clusters are made up of young, hot stars, still surrounded by the hydrogen gas from which they formed. They are slowly drifting apart from one another. Examples of open clusters include the Pleiades, which you can see in the constellation Taurus.

Globular cluster
In a globular cluster, hundreds of thousands of older, cooler stars are densely packed together. Look for M13 in the constellation of Hercules, and Omega Centuri, in Centaurus, the brightest globular cluster in the galaxy.

Omega Centauri

5 Spin the disk like a top, on a table or other flat surface.

As the disk spins, the colors blend together.

Galaxy types

Galaxies range widely in size, from dwarf galaxies containing only 100,000 stars to the massive galaxy M87, which contains 3,000 billion stars. Although most galaxies are shaped like spinning disks with spiral arms, others are elliptical, irregular, or circular in shape.

Spiral galaxies

Spiral galaxies are seen all over the sky. Barred spiral galaxies are similar, but a bar of stars stretches from the galaxy center, and the arms are attached to the bars.

Irregular galaxies

These are shapeless in appearance. The nearest are the Large and Small Magellanic Clouds, which can be seen only from the southern hemisphere.

2 Draw a third circle, 4½ in (12 cm) in diameter, on dark cardboard. Cut it out and pierce the center with a pair of compasses.

Pierce the center of the circle.

4 Cut a wooden stick 4 in (10 cm) long. Sharpen it to a point with a pencil sharpener. Push the point through the cardboard circle.

Push about 1 in (2 cm) of the stick right through the circle.

6 In a spinning, spiral galaxy, the thickly massed stars at the center are redder because they are old. The younger, hot, blue stars are found in the arms of the galaxy.

This sample of sky is representative, because the universe looks the same in all directions.

A sky crowded with galaxies

This photograph, taken by the Hubble Space Telescope, reveals hundreds of galaxies crowded into a tiny area of the universe. The photograph hints at just how many galaxies there could be.

The universe expands

There are galaxies in every direction, moving steadily apart from one another. It is as if they all originated from one point in the universe, back at the beginning of time.

You will need

- balloon
- binder clip
- silver stickers

1 Blow up the balloon a little, and fix silver stickers over its surface. These represent galaxies.

2 Blow up the balloon fully, with a binder clip handy so that no air escapes.

3 As the balloon gets bigger, the "galaxies" move apart, although they do not expand.

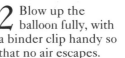

Taking it further

Once you have read this book and tried the activities, there are lots of ways to take your interest further. Visit your nearest observatory or planetarium, where demonstrations and talks will tell you more about the stars. Join your local astronomical society, and get to know other members who can help you develop your skills. After a little experience, you may be ready to work with bigger telescopes and to search the skies for more distant, fainter objects. If you would like to be a professional astronomer, then you will need to study at a college.

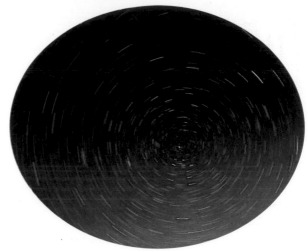

Star trails
This picture shows star trails, streaks of light on the film as the camera traces the movements of stars while they circle the pole. It requires about 30 minutes exposure.

Star photography

Astronomers often use photography to observe the stars, because photographic imaging shows things invisible to the eye even through large telescopes. The camera must be able to take long exposure photographs, where the shutter remains open for an indefinite length of time. Fully automatic cameras are battery operated and cannot be used for long exposures. Single lens reflex (SLR) 35 mm cameras are best. Balance your camera steadily on a tripod. Then point it at the stars and leave the shutter open for a couple of minutes. When you get your pictures back, you should see "streaks" of light, showing the movement of the stars across the sky.

A telephoto *(long focus)* lens like this is needed for moon photos and eclipses.

Film processing
When you have the film developed, explain to the processing firm what is on it or they may think your stars are spots on spoiled film.

Useful addresses

For futher information, contact

Hayden Planetarium
American Museum of
Natural History
Central Park West
81st Street
New York, NY 10024
212-769-5900

Griffith Observatoy
2800 E. Observatory Road
Los Angeles, CA 90027
213-664-1181

Fels Planetarium
Franklin Institute Science
Museum
20th & The Parkway
Philadelphia, PA 19103
215-448-1292

Adler Planetarium
1300 S. Lake Shore Drive
Chicago, IL 60605
312-322-0304

Charles Hayden Planetarium
Boston Science Museum
Science Park
Boston, MA 02114
617-589-0270

Abrams Planetarium
Michigan State University
East Lansing, MI 48824
517-355-4676

or contact the astronomy or physics department of your local college or university.

Glossary

Altitude
Distance between object in the sky and the horizon, measured in degrees.
Atmosphere
Layer of gases surrounding a planet; or, the outer layer of a star.
Axis
An imaginary line through the poles of an object, around which it turns.

Constellation
A group of stars,which seem to form a pattern when seen from Earth.
Eclipse
The effect caused when one object in space passes in front of another, blocking it from view.
Galaxy
A vast group of stars, held together by gravity.
Light-year
The distance traveled by light in one year—6 million million miles (9.5 million million km).

Luminosity
The amount of light produced by a star.
Magnitude
Brightness of a star or galaxy. Can be either *apparent* (as seen from Earth) or *absolute* (as if measured from a standard distance of 32.5 light-years).
Nebula
Cloud of gas and dust in space.
Orbit
Path that one object in space takes around another.

Phases
Apparent changes in shape of a moon or planet, seen from Earrh. Caused as different amounts of their sunlit sides become visible.
Planet
A rocky or gaseous body in orbit around a star.
Star
A luminous and fiercely hot ball of gas, constantly generating energy through nuclear fusion reactions.
Universe
Everything there is.

Index

Acknowledgments

DK would like to thank the following people
for their kind help in the production of this book:

All the young astronomers: Mattie Crowley, Carlene Davis, James Hall, Annabelle Halls, Olivia King, Anthony McNally, Tom Ross, Melissa Simmonds, and Lewis Wong. Special thanks to Rebecca Johns and Fiona Robertson
The publisher would like to thank the following for their kind permission to reproduce the photographs:
l=left, r=right, t=top, c=center, a=above, b=below

Bridgeman Art Library: Private Collection Albrecht Durer (1471–1528) 8cr; **Carnegie Institution of Washington:** 23 br; **Galaxy Picture Library:** Stan Armstrong 22tl, Gordon Garradd 5c, 30br, Y Hirose 36tr, NASA 16bl, Robin Scagell 9tc, 10cl, 18c, 20 tl, 29tr, 33tr, STScI 28bla, 35tr, Michael Stecker 34clb, Paul Sutherland 32tl; **Images Colour Library:** 8cl, bc; **NASA** 9tr, br, 14cl, bl, 17tr, 18bl, 21tl, tr, tc, 23tr, 24tr, 34tl, bc; **National**

Maritime Museum, London: 8br, 9tl; **Natural History Museum, London:** 33cra; **Science Photo Library**: NASA 16tc, tcr, tr; **Telegraph Colour Library:** 18tr

Planet statistics

MERCURY
Diameter	3,032 miles (4,878 km)
Average distance from Sun	36 million miles (57.9 million km)
Orbital period (year)	88 Earth days

VENUS
Diameter	7,520 miles (12,102 km)
Average distance from Sun	67.2 million miles (108.2 million km)
Orbital period (year)	224.7 Earth days

EARTH
Diameter	7,928 miles (12,756 km)
Average distance from Sun	93 million miles (149.6 million km)
Orbital period (year)	365.25 days

MARS
Diameter	4,217 miles (6,786 km)
Average distance from Sun	141.6 million miles (227.9 million km)
Orbital period (year)	687 Earth days

JUPITER
Diameter	88,865 miles (142,984 km)
Average distance from Sun	483.7 million miles (778.3 million km)
Orbital period (year)	11.86 Earth years

SATURN
Diameter	74,914 miles (120,536 km)
Average distance from Sun	886.9 million miles (1,427 million km)
Orbital period (year)	29.46 Earth years

URANUS
Diameter	31,770 miles (51,118 km)
Average distance from Sun	1,784 million miles (2,871 million km)
Orbital period (year)	84 Earth years

NEPTUNE
Diameter	30,782 miles (49,528 km)
Average distance from Sun	2,795 million miles (4,498 million km)
Orbital period (year)	164.8 Earth years

PLUTO
Diameter	1,429 miles (2,300 km)
Average distance from Sun	3,675 million miles (5,913.5 million km)
Orbital period (year)	248.5 Earth years

Planet spotting

The planets you can see with the naked eye look like stars, but over a period of weeks you'll see that they move against the fixed starry background.

MERCURY
Always too close to the Sun for safe viewing. Best seen when farthest east or west of the Sun, morning or evening twice a year.

VENUS
Brightest planet. Often mistaken for a UFO. Best seen morning or evenings.

MARS
Known by its reddish color.

JUPITER
Second brightest planet. Its slow orbit around the Sun means it is sometimes seen all night for months. Look for its four biggest moons.

SATURN
Takes over 29 years to orbit the Sun, so it is in or out of view for long periods. The planet's rings are only clear through a good telescope. Look for the largest satellite, Titan.

URANUS
Only visible as a faint dot of light. Not a good object for viewing by telescope. Surface details seen only with very large telescopes.

NEPTUNE
Even the largest telescopes show no surface detail of this planet.

PLUTO
Too distant for an amateur to spot.

Eclipses

Total lunar	Where visible
Jan 21, 2000	The Americas, southwest Europe, West Africa
Jul 16, 2000	Australia, Southeast Asia
Jan 9, 2001	Africa, Asia, Europe
May 16, 2003	South and Central America
Nov 9, 2003	The Americas

Total solar	Where visible
Aug 11, 1999	Europe
Jun 21, 2001	South Atlantic, South Africa
Dec 4, 2002	Southern Africa, South Pacific, Australia
Nov 23, 2003	South Pacific, Antarctica

MT. PLEASANT BRANCH